Primary Geography

Teacher's Book 4 Movement

Stephen Scoffham | Colin Bridge

Geography in the primary school

Geography is the study of the Earth's surface. It helps children understand the human and physical forces which shape the environment. Children are naturally interested in their immediate surroundings. They also want to know about places beyond their direct experience. Geography is uniquely placed to satisfy this curiosity.

Geographical enquiries

Geography is an enquiry-led subject that seeks to answer fundamental questions such as:

- Where is this place?
- What is this place like (and why)?
- How and why is it changing?
- How does this place compare with other places?
- How and why are places connected?

These questions involve not only finding out about the natural processes which have shaped our environment, they also involve finding out how people have responded to them. Studying this interaction at a range of scales from the local to the global and asking questions about what is happening in the world around us lie at the heart of both academic and school geography.

Geographical perspectives

Geographical perspectives offer a uniquely powerful way of seeing the world. Since the time of the Ancient Greeks geographers have been attempting to chronicle and interpret their surroundings. One way of seeing links and connections is to think in terms of key ideas. Three concepts which geographers have found particularly useful in a range of settings are place, space and scale.

- Place focuses attention on the environment.
- Space focuses attention on location.
- Scale introduces a change in perspective that enables us to link the local and the global.

A layer of secondary concepts such as patterns, change and movement lie beneath these fundamental organising ideas and provide a way of further enhancing our understanding.

As they conduct their enquiries and investigations geographers make use of a number of specific skills. Foremost among these are mapwork and the ability to represent spatial information. The use of maps, charts, diagrams, tables, sketches and other cartographic techniques come under the more general heading of 'graphicacy' and are a distinguishing feature of geographical thinking. As more and more information has come to be represented electronically, the use of computers and other electronic applications has been championed by geography educators.

Geography in primary schools offers children from the earliest ages a fascinating window onto the contemporary world. The challenge for educators is to find ways of providing experiences and selecting content that will help children develop an increasingly deep understanding.

Collins Primary Geography

Collins Primary Geography is a complete programme for pupils in the primary school and can be used as a structure for teaching geography from ages 5-11. It consists of five pupil books and supporting teacher's guides with notes and copymasters. There is one pupil book at Key Stage 1 and four pupil books at Key Stage 2. There is also a supporting DVD for each Key Stage.

Aims

The overall aim of the programme is to inspire children with an enthusiasm for geography and to empower them as learners. The underlying principles include a commitment to international understanding in a more equitable world, a concern for the future welfare of the planet and a recognition that creativity, hope and optimism play a fundamental role in lasting learning. Three different dimensions – connecting to the environment, connecting to each other and connecting to ourselves – are explored throughout the programme in different contexts and at a range of scales. We believe that learning to think geographically in the broadest meaning of the term will help children make wise decisions in the future as they grow into adulthood.

Structure

Collins Primary Geography provides full coverage of the English National Curriculum requirements. Each pupil book covers a balanced range of themes and topics and includes case studies with a more precise focus:

- Book 1 and 2 *World around us* introduces pupils to the world at both a local and global scale.
- Book 3 *Investigation* encourages pupils to conduct their own research and enquiries.
- Book 4 *Movement* considers how movement affects the physical and human environment.
- Book 5 *Change* includes case studies on how places alter and develop.
- Book 6 *Issues* introduces more complex ideas to do with the environment and sustainability.

Although the books are not limited to a specific year band, Book 3 will be particularly suitable for Year 3 children. Similarly, Book 4 is focused on Year 4 children. However it is also possible to trace themes from one book to another. The programme is structured in such a way that key themes are revisited making it possible to investigate a specific topic in greater depth if required.

Investigations

Enquiries and investigations are an important part of pupils' work in primary geography. Asking questions and searching for answers can help children develop key knowledge, understanding and skills. Fieldwork is time consuming when it involves travelling to distant locations, but local area work can be equally effective. Many of the exercises in *Collins Primary Geography* focus on the classroom, school building and local environment. We believe that such activities can have a seminal role in promoting long term positive attitudes towards sustainability and the environment.

Places, themes and skills

Each book is divided into ten units giving a balance between places, themes and skills.

Places

There are locality studies throughout each book and studies of specific places from the UK, Europe and other continents. These studies illustrate how people interact with their physical surroundings in a constantly changing world. The places have been selected so that by the end of the scheme, children will be familiar with a balanced range of reference points from around the world. They should also have developed an increasingly sophisticated locational framework which will enable them to place their new knowledge in context.

Themes

Physical geography is covered in the initial three units of each book which focus on planet Earth, water and weather. Human geography is considered in units on settlements, work and travel. There is also a unit specifically devoted to the urban and rural environment and human impact on the natural world. This is a very important aspect of modern geography and a key topic for schools generally.

Skills

Maps and plans are introduced in context to convey information about the places which are being studied. The books contain maps at scales which range from the local to global and use a range of techniques which children can emulate. Charts, diagrams and other graphical devices are included throughout. Fieldwork is strongly emphasised and all the books include projects and investigations which can be conducted in the local environment.

Information technology

Geography has always been closely associated with information technology. The way in which computers can be used for recording and processing information is illustrated in each of the books. Satellite images are included together with information from data handling packages. Oblique and vertical aerial photographs are included as sources of evidence.

Cross-curricular links

The different units in *Collins Primary Geography* can be easily linked with other subjects. The physical geography units have natural synergies with themes from sciences, as do the units on the environment. Local area studies overlap with work in history. Furthermore, the opportunities for promoting the core subjects are particularly strong. Each lesson is supported by discussion questions and many of the investigations involve written work in different modes and registers.

Places, themes and skills

Places and Themes	Book 3 Units	Book 4 Units	Book 5 Units	Book 6 Units
Planet Earth	Landscapes	Coasts	Seas and oceans	Restless Earth
Water	Water around us	Rivers	Wearing away the land	Drinking water
Weather	Weather worldwide	Weather patterns	The seasons	Local weather
Settlements	Villages	Towns	Cities	Planning issues
Work and travel	Travel	Food and shops	Jobs	Transport
Environment	Caring for the countryside	Caring for towns	Pollution	Conservation
United Kingdom	Scotland	Northern Ireland	Wales	England
Europe	France	Germany	Greece	Europe
North and South America	South America *Chile*	North America *The Rocky Mountains*	North America *Jamaica*	South America *The Amazon*
Asia and Africa	Asia *India*	Asia *UAE*	Africa *Kenya*	Asia *Singapore*

Layout of the units

Each book is divided into ten units composed of three lessons. In the opening units pupils are introduced to key themes such as water, weather, settlement and the environment at increasing levels of complexity. The following units focus on places from around the UK, Europe and other continents. The overall aim is to provide a balanced coverage of geography.

Unit title
Identifies the focus of the unit and suggests links and connections to other subjects.

Lesson title
Identifies the theme of the lesson. The supporting copymaster also uses this title which makes it easy to identify.

Enquiry question
Suggests opportunities for open-ended investigations and practical activities.

Key word panel
Highlights key geographical words and terms which will be used during the lesson.

Introductory text
Introduces the topic in a graded text of around 100 words.

Discussion panel
Consists of three questions designed to draw pupils into the topic and to stimulate discussion. The first question often involves simple comprehension, the second question involves reasoning and the third question introduces a human element which helps to relate the topic to the child's own experience.

Graphics
Graphical devices ranging from maps to satellite images amplify the topic.

Data Bank
Provides extra information to engage children and encourage them to find out more for themselves.

Mapwork exercise
Indicates how the lesson can be developed through atlas and mapwork.

Investigation panel
Suggests a practical activity which will help pupils consolidate their understanding.

Summary panel
Indicates the knowledge and understanding covered in the unit.

Copymasters
Each lesson has a supporting copymaster which can be found in pages 30-59 of this book.

Layout of the units

Enquiry question

Lesson title

Key word panel

Unit title

Discussion panel

Data Bank

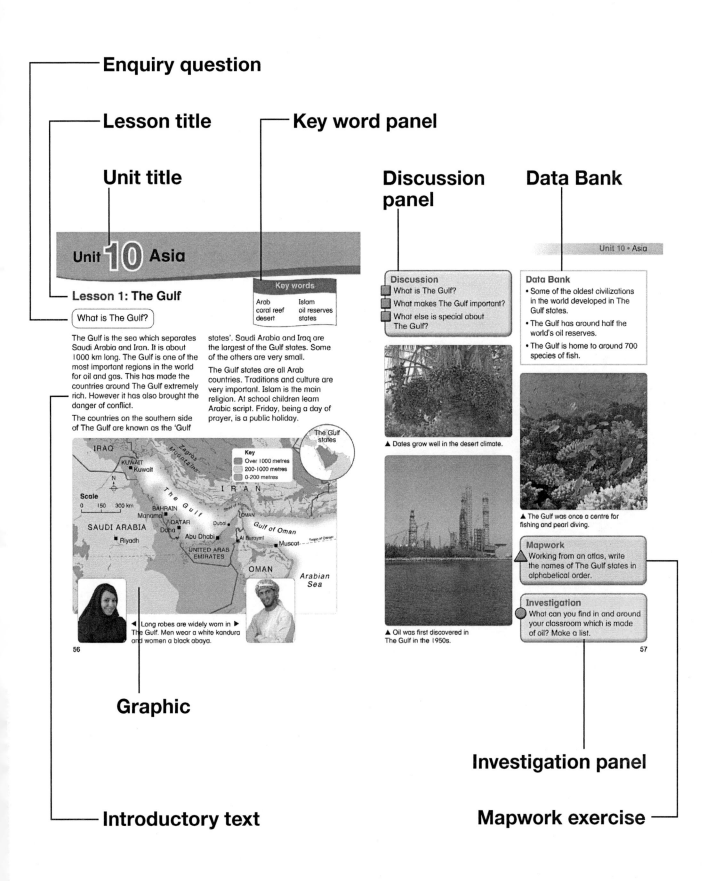

Unit **10** Asia

Lesson 1: The Gulf

What is The Gulf?

The Gulf is the sea which separates Saudi Arabia and Iran. It is about 1000 km long. The Gulf is one of the most important regions in the world for oil and gas. This has made the countries around The Gulf extremely rich. However it has also brought the danger of conflict.

The countries on the southern side of The Gulf are known as the 'Gulf

states'. Saudi Arabia and Iraq are the largest of the Gulf states. Some of the others are very small.

The Gulf states are all Arab countries. Traditions and culture are very important. Islam is the main religion. At school children learn Arabic script. Friday, being a day of prayer, is a public holiday.

Key words

Arab	Islam
coral reef	oil reserves
desert	states

◄ Long robes are widely worn in ▶ The Gulf. Men wear a white kandura and women a black abaya.

56

Discussion
- What is The Gulf?
- What makes The Gulf important?
- What else is special about The Gulf?

▲ Dates grow well in the desert climate.

▲ Oil was first discovered in The Gulf in the 1950s.

Unit 10 • Asia

Data Bank
- Some of the oldest civilizations in the world developed in The Gulf states.
- The Gulf has around half the world's oil reserves.
- The Gulf is home to around 700 species of fish.

▲ The Gulf was once a centre for fishing and pearl diving.

Mapwork
Working from an atlas, write the names of The Gulf states in alphabetical order.

Investigation
What can you find in and around your classroom which is made of oil? Make a list.

57

Graphic

Investigation panel

Introductory text

Mapwork exercise

Lesson planning

Collins Primary Geography has been designed to support both whole school and individual lesson planning. As you devise your schemes and work out lesson plans you may find it helpful to ask the following questions. For example, have you:

- Given children a range of entry points which will engage their enthusiasm and capture their imagination?
- Used a range of teaching strategies which cater for pupils who learn in different ways?
- Thought about using games as a teaching device?
- Explored the ways that stories or personal accounts might be integrated with the topic?
- Considered the opportunities for practical activities and fieldwork enquiries?
- Encouraged pupils to use globes and maps where appropriate?
- Considered whether to include a global dimension?
- Checked to see whether you are challenging rather than reinforcing stereotypes?
- Checked on links to suitable websites, particularly with respect to research?
- Made use of ICT to record findings or analyse information?

- Made links to other subjects where there is a natural overlap?
- Promoted geography alongside literacy skills especially in talking and writing?
- Taken advantage of the opportunities for presentations and class displays?
- Ensured that the pupils are developing geographical skills and meaningful subject knowledge?
- Clarified the knowledge, skills and concepts that will underpin the unit?
- Identified appropriate learning outcomes or given pupils the opportunity to identify their own ones?

These questions are offered as prompts which may help you to generate stimulating and lively lessons. There is clear evidence that when geography is fun and pupils enjoy what they are doing it can lead to lasting learning. Striking a balance between light-hearted delivery and serious intent is part of the craft of being a teacher.

Misconceptions

There is a growing body of research which helps practitioners to understand more about how children learn primary geography and the barriers and challenges that they commonly encounter. The way that young children assume that the physical environment was created by people was first highlighted by Jean Piaget. The importance and significance of early childhood misconceptions was further illuminated by Howard Gardner. More recent research has considered how children develop their understanding of maps and places. Children's ideas about other countries and their attitudes to other nationalities form another very important line of enquiry. Some key readings are listed in the references on page 15.

Lesson summary

The table below provides an overview of the lessons in *Collins Primary Geography Pupil Book 4.* Individual schools may want to adapt the lessons and associated activities according to their particular needs and circumstances.

Theme	Unit	Lesson 1	Lesson 2	Lesson 3
Planet Earth	Coasts	The seashore	Shaping the coast	Exploring the coast
Water	Rivers	Describing rivers	Rivers matter	Managing rivers
Weather	Weather patterns	Extreme weather	Weather forecasts	Recording the weather
Settlements	Towns	Understanding towns	The origin of towns	Town life
Work and travel	Food and shops	Farms and food	From farm to supermarket	Local shops
Environment	Caring for towns	Old and new buildings	Making improvements	Comparing places
United Kingdom	Northern Ireland	Introducing Northern Ireland	Living in Northern Ireland	A journey to Londonderry
Europe	Germany	Knowing Germany	The Ruhr: An industrial region	Living in Dinslaken
North and South America	North America	Introducing North America	Finding out about Canada	Crossing the Rockies
Asia and Africa	Asia	The Gulf	Introducing the United Arab Emirates	Exploring the United Arab Emirates

Studying the local area

The local area is the immediate vicinity around the school and the home. It consists of three different components: the school building, the school grounds, and local streets and buildings. By studying their local area, children will learn about the different features which make their environment distinctive and how it attains a specific character. When they are familiar with their own area, they will then be able to make meaningful comparisons with more distant places.

There are many opportunities to support the lessons outlined in *Collins Primary Geography* with practical local area work. First-hand experience is fundamental to good practice in geography teaching, is a clear requirement in the programme of study and has been highlighted in guidance to Ofsted inspectors. The local area can be used not only to develop ideas from human geography but also to illustrate physical and environmental themes. The checklist below illustrates some of the features which could be identified and studied.

Physical geography	Human geography
Hill, valley, cliff, mountain, rock, slope, soil, wood	Origins of settlements, land use and economic activity
River, stream, pond, lake, estuary, coast	House, cottage, terrace, flat, housing estate
Slopes, rock, soil, plants and other small-scale features	Roads, stations, harbours
Local weather and site conditions	Shops, factories and offices
	Fire, police, ambulance, health services
	Library, museum, park, leisure centre

All work in the local area involves collecting and analysing information. An important way in which this can be achieved is through the use of maps and plans. Other techniques include annotated drawings, bar charts, tables and reports. There will also be opportunities for the children to make presentations in class and perhaps to the rest of the school in assemblies.

Studying places in the UK and wider world

Collins Primary Geography Pupil Book 4 contains studies of the following places in the UK and wider world. Place studies focus on small scale environments and everyday life. By considering people and describing their surroundings, the information is presented at a scale and in a manner which relates particularly well to children. Research shows that pupils tend to reach a peak of friendliness towards other countries and nations at about the age of ten. It is important to capitalise on this educationally and to challenge prejudices and stereotypes.

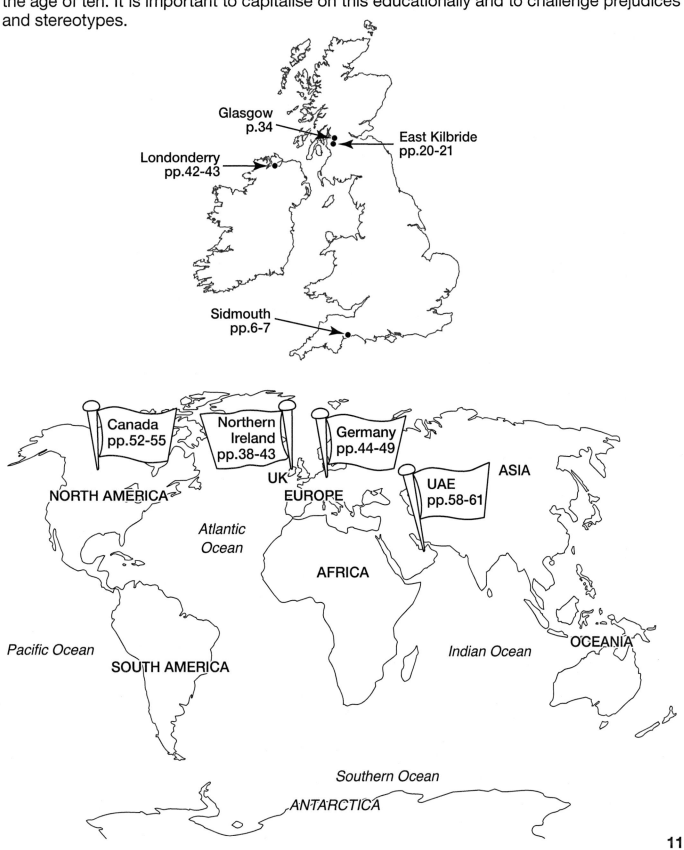

Differentiation and progression

Collins Primary Geography sets out to provide access to the curriculum for children of all abilities. It is structured so that children can respond to and use the material in a variety of ways. Within each unit there is a range of exercises and discussion questions. This means activities can be selected which are appropriate to individual circumstances.

Differentiation by outcome

Each lesson starts with an introductory text and linked discussion questions which are designed to capture the children's imagination and draw them into the topic. There are opportunities for slower learners to relate the material to their own experience. More able children will be able to consider the underlying geographical concepts. The pace and range of the discussion can be controlled to suit the needs of the class or group.

Differentiation by task

The mapwork and investigation exercises can be modified according to the pupils' ability levels. Teachers may decide to complete some of the tasks as class exercises or help slower learners by working through the first part of an exercise with them. Classroom assistants could also use the lessons with individual children or small groups. More able children could be given extension tasks. Ideas and suggestions for extending each lesson are provided in the information on individual units (pages 16-25).

Differentiation by process

Children of all abilities benefit from exploring their environment and conducting their own investigations. The investigation activities include many suggestions for direct experience and first-hand learning. Work in the local area can overcome the problems of written communication by focusing on concrete events. There are also opportunities for taking photographs and conducting surveys as well as for making lists, diagrams and written descriptions.

Progression

The themes, language and complexity of the material have been graded to provide progression between each title. However, the gradient between different books is deliberately shallow. This makes it possible for the books to be used interchangeably by different year groups or within mixed ability classes. The way that this might work can be illustrated by considering a sample unit. For instance, in Book 3 the unit on weather introduces children to hot and cold places around the world. Book 4 looks at ways of recording the weather, Book 5 focuses on the seasons and Book 6 considers local weather conditions. This approach provides opportunities for reinforcement and revisiting which will be particularly helpful for the less able child.

Assessment

Assessment is often seen as having two very different dimensions. Formative assessment is an on-going process which provides both pupils and teachers with information about the progress they are making in a piece of work. Summative assessment occurs at defined points in a child's learning and seeks to establish what they have learnt and how they are performing in relation both to their peers and to nationally agreed standards. *Collins Primary Geography* provides opportunities for both formative and summative assessment.

Formative assessment

- The discussion questions invite pupils to discuss a topic, relate it to their previous experience and consider any issues which may arise, thereby yielding information about their current knowledge and understanding.
- The mapwork exercises focus especially on developing spatial awareness and skills and will indicate the pupils' current level of ability
- The investigation activities give pupils the chance to extend their knowledge in ways that match their current abilities.

Summative assessment

- The panels at the end of each unit highlight key learning outcomes. These can be tested directly through individually designed exercises.
- The copymasters (see pages 30-59) can be used to provide additional evidence of pupil achievement. Whether used formatively or summatively they are intended to broaden and consolidate understanding.

Reporting to parents

Collins Primary Geography is structured around geographical skills, themes and place studies which become more complex from one book to another. As children work through the units they can build up a folder of work. This will include mapwork and investigations in the local area and will provide evidence of breadth, progression and achievement in geography. It will also be a useful resource when teachers report to parents about whether an individual child is above average, satisfactory, or in need of help in geography.

National curriculum reporting

There is a single attainment target for geography and other National Curriculum subjects. This simply states that

> *'By the end of each key stage, pupils are expected to know, apply and understand the matters, skills and processes specified in the relevant programme of study.'*

This means that assessment need not be an onerous burden and that evidence of pupils' achievement can be built up over an entire Key Stage. The assessment process can also inform lesson planning. Establishing what pupils have demonstrably understood helps to highlight more clearly what they still need to learn.

High quality geography

The regular reviews of geography teaching in the UK undertaken by Ofsted provide a clear guidance.

Ofsted recommendations

Ofsted recommends schools to:

- focus on developing pupils' core knowledge and sense of place.
- ensure that geography elements are clearly identified within topic based work.
- maximize opportunities for fieldwork in order to improve pupil motivation.
- make the most of new technology to enthuse pupils and provide immediacy and relevance.
- provide more opportunities for writing at length and focused reading.
- enable pupils to recognise their responsibilities as citizens.
- develop networks to share good practice.
- provide subject specific support and professional development opportunities for teachers.

Primary Geography Quality Mark

The Primary Geography Quality Mark set up by the UK Geographical Association is another measure of excellence. This provides a self-assessment framework designed to help subject leaders. There are three categories of award. The 'bronze' level recognises that lively and enjoyable geography is happening in your school, the 'silver' level recognises excellence across the school and the 'gold' level recognises excellence that is shared and embedded in the community beyond the school. The framework is divided into four separate cells (a) pupil progress and achievement (b) quality of teaching (c) behaviour and relationships (d) leadership and management. For further details see www.geography.org.uk.

Achieving accreditation for geography in school is a useful way of badging achievements and identifying targets for future improvement. The Geographical Association provides a wide range of support to help teachers with this process. In addition to an ambassador scheme and Continuing Professional Development (CPD) sessions it produces a journal for primary schools, *Primary Geography*, three time a year. Other key sources are the Geographical Association website, the *Primary Geography Handbook* and books and guides for classroom use such as *Geography Plus*.

Finding time for geography

The pressures on the school timetable and the demands of the core subjects make it hard to secure adequate time for primary geography. However, finding ways of integrating geography with mathematics and literacy can be a creative way of increasing opportunities. Geography also has a natural place in a wide range of social studies and current affairs whether local or global. It can be developed through class assemblies and extra-curricular studies. Those who are committed to thinking geographically find a surprising number of ways of developing the subject whatever the accountability regime in which they operate.

Ofsted inspections

Ofsted inspections are designed to monitor standards of teaching in schools in England and Wales. Curriculum development is an on-going process and inspectors do not always expect to see totally completed programmes. What they are looking for is evidence of carefully planned strategies which are having a positive impact on the quality of teaching. However, inspectors must also note weaknesses and highlight aspects which need attention. If curriculum development is already in hand in your school, it should receive positive support. The following checklist provides prompts which may help prepare for inspections.

1 Identify a teacher who is responsible for developing the geography curriculum.
2 Provide a regular opportunity for discussing geography teaching in staff meetings.
3 See that all members of staff are familiar with the geography curriculum.
4 Decide how geography will fit into your whole school plan.
5 Make an audit of current geography teaching resources to identify gaps and weaknesses.
6 Discuss and develop a geography policy which includes statements on overall aims, topic planning, teaching methods, resources, assessment and recording.
7 Discuss the policy with the governors.
8 Devise an action plan for geography which includes an annual review procedure.

References and further reading

Bonnett, A. (2009) *What is Geography?* London: Sage
Butt, G. (Ed.) (2011) *Geography, Education and the Future,* London: Continuum
Catling, S. and Willy, T. (2009) *Teaching Primary Geography*, Exeter: Learning Matters
DfE (2013) National Curriculum in England: Programmes of study – Key Stages 1 and 2 available at www.education.gov.uk/schools/teachingandlearning/curriculum/primary
Lucas, B. and Claxton, G. (2011) *New Kinds of Smart*, Maidenhead: Open University Press
Martin, F. (2006) *Teaching Geography in Primary Schools : Learning to live in the world*, Cambridge: Kington
Ofsted (2011) *Geography: Learning to Make a World of Difference*, London: Ofsted
Scoffham, S. (Ed.) (2010) *Primary Geography Handbook*, Sheffield: Geographical Association
Scoffham, S. (Ed.) (2013) *Teaching Geography Creatively*, London: Routledge
Wiegand, P. (2006) *Learning and Teaching with Maps*, London: Routledge

The Geographical Association

The Geographical Association (GA) provides extensive support and advice for teachers including a range of excellent publications such as the *Everyday Geography* and *Geography Plus* series. As well as holding an annual conference, the GA also produces a journal for primary practitioners, *Primary Geography*, which is published three times a year. To find out more and learn about the latest developments in geography education visit the website at www.geography.org.uk.

Unit 1: COASTS

Geographers study how the action of the waves and currents in the sea affect the seashore. Most of these changes happen slowly over many years. Young children find it hard to understand the idea of geological time as it is such a gradual process. However every so often there are dramatic cliff falls which illustrate how the coastline is altering. This can be a good opportunity to introduce the idea of change.

Lesson 1: THE SEASHORE
What is the seashore like?

The seashore is an evocative environment which attracts people of all ages. This introductory lesson establishes that coasts are remarkably different. However, while the geology and landscape may vary coasts always seem to bring people closer to the elements. As you discuss the photographs encourage the children to share their own memories and experiences of being by the seashore. This might also be the moment to consider issues to do with safety.

Mapwork *You might use the children's maps as the basis for a story in creative writing.*

Investigation *Encourage the children to extend their vocabulary by using geographical words such as beach, bay cliff and headland in their descriptions.*

Lesson 2: SHAPING THE COAST
How does the sea shape the coast?

The picture is loosely based on the West Wales coastline. The features on page 4 show how the shore is being built up. The features on page 5 show how it is being worn away. The twin processes of erosion and deposition mean that the contours of the seashore are constantly changing.

Mapwork *Headlands are dramatic coastal features and they are often marked by lighthouses. Pupils could add extra information about the headlands they have listed as an extension activity.*

Investigation *Children could be given a new booklet for geographical words at the start of the school year or use the books they started the year before. If they make careful drawings and add descriptions and annotations, these books will become a valuable record of their work and development.*

Lesson 3: EXPLORING THE COAST
How do people look after the coast?

The ways people manage the seashore are illustrated in the study of Sidmouth. After the High Street was flooded in 1921, the esplanade was repaired and the sea wall was rebuilt to a new design. The groynes near the Chit Rocks help to stop the current washing away the beach and the boulders break up the power of the waves. There are also a wide variety of facilities for visitors, some of which are shown on the map.

Mapwork *The colours on the map in the pupil book are more or less self explanatory. However, making a key is a basic mapwork skill which all children need to practice.*

What can you find on the seashore?

The diagram of the cliff and beach show some of the plants and animals that live on the seashore. The high and low water levels are marked on the diagram to indicate the zone which is regularly washed by the tide.

Investigation *The Jurassic coast was designated England's first natural World Heritage Site in 2001. It is nearly 100 miles long and contains rocks from three geological periods dating back 185 million years.*

Copymasters *See 1, 2 and 3 for linked extension exercises.*

Unit 2: RIVERS

Rivers are formed by water flowing off the land into the sea. As rivers flow downhill they grow bigger and change their character. In the upper reaches, rivers wear away the land and cut deep valleys. Nearer the mouth, they deposit sediment as mud banks. Children should understand the main elements of the process and be introduced to the appropriate geographical vocabulary. You might also explore the cross-curricular dimension using poems, music and stories.

Lesson 1: DESCRIBING RIVERS
What are the features of a river?

The story of Sammy the Salmon introduces some basic geographical vocabulary in a child friendly context. It is worth noting that children often become confused by simple terms. Thus they are likely to associate a 'channel' with a TV station rather than a river valley. Words like 'source' and 'sauce' present special difficulties.

Mapwork *This is the time to use an Ordnance Survey map of your local area. There may also be linked fieldwork opportunities.*

Investigation *Once pupils have devised their picture poems and sentences for a river they might extend this idea to other landscape features such as mountains or cliffs.*

Lesson 2: RIVERS MATTER
How do people use rivers?

The Nile was chosen for a detailed case study because it is the longest river in the world. It also provides an excellent link to historical studies of Ancient Egypt. The map and diagram illustrate two very different ways of presenting information about the Nile. They are positioned side by side for ease of comparison.

Mapwork *Identifying major world rivers and mountain ranges builds pupils' locational framework.*

Investigation *Before the children make their picture map, they will need to discuss what they are going to mark on it. Key features include the pyramids, temples, Aswan High Dam, Sudd Marshes, Kabalega Falls and Lake Victoria.*

Lesson 3: MANAGING RIVERS
How do people care for rivers?

This lesson highlights the interaction between people and the physical environment. Rivers are particularly vulnerable to pollution because they collect water from a wide area. The Environment Agency works to make rivers healthy and prevent floods.

Investigation *Discuss the work which is depicted in each of the photographs before the children undertake this activity.*

A walk along the River Thames

The sample study of the River Thames will help the children to develop an image of Britain's most well-known river. It also illustrates the potential for outdoor work using photographs and sketches to record information.

Mapwork *This open-ended map interpretation exercise could be developed through work in history and literacy.*

Copymasters *See 4, 5 and 6 for linked extension exercises.*

Unit 3: WEATHER PATTERNS

Modern life tends to isolate us from the influence of the weather. Motor vehicles, central heating and air conditioning allow us to ignore the conditions out-of-doors. Occasionally extreme weather conditions, such as droughts, floods or heavy snow, bring chaos and disruption. In less-developed countries where resources are scarce, people are more vulnerable and the weather can do terrible damage. This unit links with other subject areas, especially science and technology. The opportunities for language work and creative writing can also be explored.

Lesson 1: EXTREME WEATHER
How does the weather affect us?

In the last few decades extreme weather events have been occurring increasingly frequently. There are suggestions that this is the result of climate change. The photographs on pages 14 and 15 show a range of weather problems. There is a clear message. We are all affected by the weather wherever we may happen to live.

Investigation *This activity aims to illustrate how both natural and human life are affected by extreme weather.*

Lesson 2: WEATHER FORECASTS
Who uses the weather forecast?

It is surprising how much the weather impinges on our lives. If there are significant weather problems when you are doing this lesson you might set up a news board to show what has happened and the places most affected using information from national or local newspapers.

Investigation *The investigation explores how the weather affects different people.*

How are weather forecasts made?

Modern weather forecasts are usually extremely accurate. They are based on a huge quantity of data which is analysed by extremely powerful computers. However, there are so many factors involved that uncertainties are inevitable. Forecasts that extend beyond a period of four or five days become increasingly unreliable and are best regarded as predictions.

Mapwork *It is instructive to compare a satellite weather map with the synoptic chart which shows the position of weather fronts. The chart reveals underlying weather patterns whereas the satellite image is purely descriptive.*

Lesson 3: RECORDING THE WEATHER
How can we record the weather?

Making first-hand weather observations is an excellent fieldwork activity which can be conducted within the school grounds. If you have built up records over a number of years there will be valuable opportunities to make comparisons.

Mapwork *You might link this exercise to work on the seasons and the differences between the Northern and Southern Hemispheres.*

Investigation *Pupils could use the weather symbols from page 18 as they compile their weather records.*

Copymasters *See 7, 8 and 9 for linked extension activities.*

Unit 4: TOWNS

Before the Industrial Revolution most people in Britain lived in scattered rural communities. Now over 90 per cent of people live in towns and cities. As a result they have become increasingly dependent on public services such as water, gas and electricity. Towns vary considerably in size. They provide a greater range of shops and facilities than villages. They also act as local centres of administration and have higher-order educational facilities, such as secondary schools and colleges. In general terms the population of UK settlements falls into the following pattern:

Small village 100 - 500 people
Large village 500 - 3000 people
Small town 3000 - 10,000 people

Large town 10,000 - 100,000 people
City 100,000 - 1,000,000 or more people

Lesson 1: UNDERSTANDING TOWNS
What are the features of a town?

East Kilbride was designated as Scotland's first new town in 1947. It has grown from being a village to a modern town with a population of 74,000 people. The planners who designed East Kildbride tried to include the facilities which they thought people needed. Pupils are invited to think about these in this lesson.

Mapwork *The mapwork exercise gives children the chance to practice identifying grid squares as they locate specific features of the town centre.*

Investigation *You could develop this activity into a study of land use patterns which will reveal the enormous amount of space given to transport.*

Lesson 2: THE ORIGIN OF TOWNS
How did towns begin?

Towns develop for a number of different and overlapping reasons in which geography, history and chance all play a significant part. Sometimes one key factor plays a dominant role. The photographs illustrate some of the possibilities. Pupils may be able to think of other examples.

Mapwork *As pupils find out how their local town has developed they will naturally be drawn into thinking about its history.*

Investigation *This activity may reveal how towns which were once important have been overtaken by others which have proved more successful.*

Lesson 3: TOWN LIFE
How does a town work?

We tend to take public services for granted yet life quickly grinds to a halt if any of them breaks down. The diagram shows some of the main services on which a town depends and suggests through visual representation how they are all interdependent.

Mapwork *In order to decide on the location of a litter bin, pupils will need to find out where litter bins are currently placed. They will also need to consider questions to do with access and the distance from individual houses.*

Investigation *Pupils might use their photographs to make a short PowerPoint presentation about the services which help a town to function.*

Copymasters *See 10, 11 and 12 for linked extension exercises.*

Unit 5: FOOD AND SHOPS

There have been great changes in food production and distribution over the past 50 years. On the land the increased use of machinery, fertilisers and insecticides has led to much higher yields and greater productivity. However intensive farming is also leading to soil degradation and the loss of biodiversity. At the same time there have also been great changes in retailing. Small shops in villages and suburban side streets have been replaced by out-of-town supermarkets and internet shopping. The effect that this is having on traditional town centres is a matter of increasing social and economic interest.

Lesson 1: FARMS AND FOOD
Where does our food come from?

Children tend to have a rather romantic view of farming. Poems, songs and fairy tales overlook the fact that growing crops and looking after animals is a demanding occupation requiring long hours of repetitive work. This lesson alerts pupils to the way that farming is an economic activity which responds to geographical forces.

Mapwork *To complete this exercise pupils could use an internet distance calculator but actually measuring the distance from an atlas map is an excellent way of developing their ability to use scales and scale bars.*

Investigation *The investigation will highlight the way we depend on food that has been grown in other countries.*

Lesson 2: FROM FARM TO SUPERMARKET
How does food get to supermarkets?

Shops obtain their goods from a wide variety of different sources and are the last point in a lengthy chain of production. However, as these processes are hidden from view, many children are not aware that they happen. The supply of fruit and vegetables makes a particularly interesting case study. Seasonal variations can be more or less eliminated by obtaining supplies from farms in different parts of the world.

Mapwork *The main route from Turkey to the UK passes east of the Alps through Belgrade and Vienna.*

Investigation *This study of bananas might be used alongside the unit on the Caribbean in pupil book 3.*

Lesson 3: LOCAL SHOPS
Investigating local shops

First-hand investigations of local shops offers pupils the opportunity to consolidate their understanding of the chain. You will need to see that they are familiar with specialist names such as baker, butcher and chemist before they undertake any investigation. The usual fieldwork health and safety considerations apply.

Mapwork *Using a large scale local map is an important part of this study and will help pupils to see patterns and connections.*

Investigation *Many schools will be in easy walking distance of a shopping precinct even if they do not have a local street.*

Copymasters *See 13, 14 and 15 for linked extension exercises.*

Unit 6: CARING FOR TOWNS

Interest in the urban environment was boosted by the widespread destruction of buildings during the Second World War. Since then, people have become more and more concerned about conserving our heritage. There are about 440,000 buildings in England which are 'listed' as being of special architectural or historical merit. Examples range from old telephone boxes and the Palm House at Kew Gardens to the Jodrell Bank Radio Telescope in Cheshire. The list is split up into three categories:

Grade I Buildings of 'exceptional interest' such as castles, cathedrals and large country houses.
Grade II* About 20,000 buildings of 'more than special interest'.
Grade II Most buildings put up before 1840 as well as outstanding buildings of more recent date.

Lesson 1: OLD AND NEW BUILDINGS
What happens to old buildings?
The photograph of the block of flats being demolished is intended to capture the children's interest and to promote discussion. Many of the high-rise flats put up in the 1960s were badly built and have proved unsuitable for the people who live in them. You might discuss which buildings are worth preserving. Are there any general criteria?
Mapwork *The windmill in the photograph has a tapering round tower. Children might add windows and other features as they like.*
Investigation *You will be able to find out about local listed buildings either from the internet or by visiting your local council planning department.*

Lesson 2: MAKING IMPROVEMENTS
How can places be improved?
This lesson begins by considering an urban improvement scheme and requires pupils to look carefully at a plan. One of the key ideas here is that people make choices about the kind of environment they want to create. After consulting local people the council put benches, paths and trees in Cochrane Street. You might want to discuss other options to illustrate the range of possibilities.
Improvement schemes
The improvement schemes focus on new developments, most of which are to do with mitigating the effect of traffic.
Mapwork *You might use an empty site in the local area for the mapwork exercise.*
Investigation *When they complete their reports there is no reason why pupils have to agree that the changes shown in the drawings really are improvements.*

Lesson 3: COMPARING PLACES
Which place is best?
This lesson draws attention to the quality of the local environment and the features which contribute to its character. The things we see around us reflect the complexities of interacting social, economic, cultural and environmental forces. Local streetwork is a good starting point.
Mapwork *Pupils could work in groups and make presentations of their ideas to the rest of the class.*
Investigation *The report on school improvements might lead to a discussion with teachers, governors and others who have a responsibility for running and maintaining the school.*

Copymasters *See 16, 17 and 18 for linked extension exercises.*

Unit 7: NORTHERN IRELAND

Northern Ireland was created in 1921 when the Republic of Ireland gained independence. It is one of the four countries of the UK and is sometimes referred to as Ulster. If your school is in Northern Ireland you might use this unit to help teach some of the specific requirements of the Northern Ireland curriculum. If your school is in another area, the maps, photographs and text will serve to enlarge the children's ideas of the UK.

Lesson 1: INTRODUCING NORTHERN IRELAND
What is Northern Ireland like?

In introducing this lesson make sure the children understand that Ireland is divided into two parts. The Republic of Ireland (Eire) covers central and southern areas and is predominantly Catholic. Northern Ireland is a much smaller area with a strong Protestant community. Conflicts between Irish Catholics and the Protestants have a long history and have yet to be fully resolved.

Mapwork *Once pupils have found out ferry routes they could plan journeys from places in different parts of Britain such as Plymouth and Aberdeen.*

Investigation *See if the children can find photographs which challenge stereotypes as well as images of attractive or famous places.*

Lesson 2: LIVING IN NORTHERN IRELAND
What is it like to live in Northern Ireland?

Apart from Belfast and a few other cities, most parts of Northern Ireland are deeply rural. The portrait of the O'Neill family is designed to give pupils an image of everyday life in a country area. The whole family is involved in running the farm. One of the parents has a part-time job to provide extra income. The children live in a tranquil environment but they have to travel by bus to get to school. Ballynahone Bog, a few kilometres from their home, is a raised lowland peat bog that supports a rich variety of wildlife especially birds, butterflies and dragonflies. It is the largest nature reserve in Northern Ireland.

Lesson 3: A JOURNEY TO LONDONDERRY
What might you see on a journey to Londonderry?

The O'Neills' journey to Londonderry is shown in cartoon style to introduce an element of variety and to give the children a model to copy if they want to portray journeys of their own. If you are doing a project on 'movement', 'travel' or 'journeys' you could integrate this lesson into your work. There are also opportunities to focus on environmental issues.

Mapwork *The picture map might take a number of different forms. It could consist of a trail or route annotated with illustrations of key features. It might be a series of simple pictures on a long strip of card showing the sequence of landmarks with notes on distances between them. It could be a composite picture which shows the relationships between places in an artistic manner. If you provide pupils with examples of historical maps these will provide valuable models and help to broaden their thinking.*

Investigation *As well as having high ecological value, peat bogs are also yielding valuable archaeological evidence as increasing numbers of artefacts and remains are uncovered.*

Copymasters *See 19, 20 and 21 for linked extension exercises.*

Unit 8: GERMANY

Germany is one of the largest and most important countries in Europe. It occupies a central position between France in the west and Poland in the east. Many areas are densely populated with large towns and cities especially along the River Rhine. In 1945, after the Second World War, Germany was divided into two parts. West Germany evolved as a major economic power and one of the founder members of the European Union. East Germany developed in a different way under communism. The two countries were reunited in 1990 but social, economic and environmental problems have taken a very long time to resolve.

Lesson 1: KNOWING GERMANY
What is Germany like?

Many children will already have images of Germany either because they have been there themselves or have heard about it from relatives. They may also have gathered unbalanced impressions from television films, books and stories. More accurate images can be developed through the material in this lesson.

Mapwork *By drawing their own maps of Germany pupils will begin to appreciate some its key geographical features.*

Investigation *Children will need to conduct their own research about the Rhine valley before they can make their zigzag books.*

Lesson 2: THE RUHR: AN INDUSTRIAL REGION
What is the Ruhr like?

This lesson begins by establishing where the Ruhr is in relation to the UK. As they find out about Dominic's journey pupils might work out the route which they would take from their own part of the UK.

Dinslaken: A town in the Ruhr

The Ruhr is a region in northwestern Germany which takes its name from one of the rivers that flows into the Rhine. The Ruhr became the centre of Germany's manufacturing industry in the nineteenth and twentieth centuries. Local supplies of coal and iron provided raw materials for heavy industries such as iron, steel, chemicals, textiles and armaments. The Rhine and other waterways were used for transport. As these industries have declined new activities have taken their place. Dinslaken is a typical example of the changes that have taken place.

Mapwork *Pupils could either use the map on page 46 or find one of their own on the internet.*

Investigation *This activity will draw children into finding out the history of the Ruhr and its importance in the past.*

Lesson 3: LIVING IN DINSLAKEN
What is it like to visit Dinslaken?

The focus on everyday life is designed to help children learn about Germany in terms of human as well as physical geography.

Changes and differences

Although Dinslaken forms part of the Ruhr it is close to open countryside. The old industrial areas are being transformed through investment in cultural and leisure activities. The improved living conditions and the location of the Ruhr at the centre of the European Union is once again making it attractive to industry.

Mapwork *This exercise highlights the fact that there are many jobs in the Ruhr towns, many of which require special skills.*

Investigation *The timeline is one way of tracing the changing fortunes of the town.*

Copymasters *See 22, 23 and 24 for linked extension activities*

Information on the units

Unit 9: NORTH AMERICA

North America is bounded by the Arctic, Pacific and Atlantic oceans. It is the world's third largest continent by area and the fourth largest by population. Greenland and the Rocky Mountains are the most dominant physical features. Most of the urban areas (apart from Mexico City) are on the coast. Historical and geographical factors have combined to create different regions within North America. Canada and the USA are vast English-speaking countries with advanced economies. Mexico and the other countries to the south form a block of less affluent Spanish-speaking countries. In the Caribbean there is a group of island nations with colonial links to western Europe and a mixed population that includes considerable numbers of Africans.

Lesson 1: INTRODUCING NORTH AMERICA
What is North America like?

Many pupils will have images of North America derived from films such as Westerns and television programmes. You could begin this lesson by tapping into what the children know. Extend their understanding by interrogating the text, photographs and map on pages 50 and 51. Are there any places which they have heard of already?

Mapwork *Pupils will need to look at an atlas to find the names of the states. They might just include those which begin with a vowel.*

Investigation *Try to see that the display represents both physical and human geography. It will also be important to include photographs of issues – both environmental and social.*

Lesson 2: FINDING OUT ABOUT CANADA
What is Canada like?

Canada is 40 times the size of the UK but only has about half the population. It has been settled for thousands of years by aboriginal people now collectively known as the First Nations. British and French colonists began to arrive from the fifteenth century onwards. Most of the land was ceded to the English in the eighteenth century but the French influence still persists in Quebec where French is the official language.

Mapwork *Countries with only one land border include South Korea, Papua New Guinea, Ireland and the UK.*

Investigation *See that pupils are able to answer the questions they devise as ambiguities are likely to arise.*

Lesson 3: CROSSING THE ROCKIES
What is it like to cross the Rockies?

The Trans-Canada highway is one of the longest road systems in the world. Work started in 1950 but the highway was not completed till 1971. The route between the Atlantic the Pacific oceans involves ferry crossings as well as mountain passes.

Mapwork *Note that when the children draw their maps there are parallel or alternative routes in many places.*

Investigation *There are numerous websites about the highway for children to explore, some of which include webcams.*

Copymasters *See 25, 26 and 27 for linked extension exercises.*

Information on the units

Unit 10: ASIA

Asia is a vast land mass with many different geographical regions. The area around The Gulf forms a distinct desert region within Asia and is the focus for this unit. The northern side of The Gulf is dominated by Iran. On the southern side there are a number of Arab states which are united through religion, language and culture. All these states have huge reserves of oil and gas. The revenue from these resources has led to very rapid development across the region over the last 50 years. Modern cities with hi-tech buildings have been constructed on a massive scale, especially along the coast. Large numbers of migrant workers have been recruited to make up for the shortage of local labour. The geographical location of The Gulf between Africa, Europe and Asia and its links by sea to the Indian Ocean now mean it is in a strong position to serve as a world centre for trade and communications.

Lesson 1: THE GULF
What is The Gulf?

This lesson focuses on the Gulf states. As well as highlighting their common heritage and traditions, the text and photographs introduce social and economic factors.

Mapwork *This exercise will lead children to interrogate the map and identify some of the key geographical features of the region.*

Investigation *Oil is crucially important in contemporary life. Not only does it provide fuel for cars, planes and heating systems but, when turned into plastic and nylon, it is a component of many manufactured goods.*

Lesson 2: INTRODUCING THE UNITED ARAB EMIRATES
What is the United Arab Emirates like?

This lesson introduces pupils to the UAE and focuses especially on the mixture of modernity and tradition which is found throughout the region. There are opportunities to find out more about Islam art and culture through linked studies in art and religious studies. Traditional and modern sports is another theme which could be explored in greater depth.

Mapwork *This exercise will help pupils comprehend the enormous height of the Burj Khalifa skyscraper.*

Investigation *The links between the Gulf states and other Muslim countries is expressed symbolically in their flags.*

Lesson 3: EXPLORING THE UNITED ARAB EMIRATES
The UAE today

The physical and human geography of the UAE is explored in this lesson. Links with other countries form a sub theme along with environmental issues. The inter-relationships between people and their surroundings – a fundamental idea in geography – is exemplified in a number of different ways. This provide a fitting theme for the last lesson in this pupil book.

Mapwork *Pupils might draw straight lines from the UAE to the countries which buy the oil. Alternatively they could identify the sea route, perhaps calculating the distance at the same time.*

Investigation *There are some good educational websites which explore the idea of environmental footprints and which allow children to make their own calculations for food miles.*

Copymasters *See 28, 29 and 30 for linked extension exercises.*

Copymaster matrix

Unit	Copymaster	Description
Coasts	1 The seashore	The children colour two outline pictures of the seashore and make two drawings of their own.
	2 Shaping the coast	Pupils colour an outline drawing of the seashore using a key.
	3 Exploring the coast	The children add labels and colour a map of Sidmouth.
Rivers	1 Describing rivers	Working from a drawing, the children pick out six different features of a river valley.
	2 Rivers matter	Pupils colour a map of the River Nile and identify key features along its course.
	3 Managing rivers	The children make a set of drawings to show how people look after rivers.
Weather patterns	1 Extreme weather	Working from a word bank, pupils describe three different types of extreme weather.
	2 Weather forecasts	Children decide what clothes to take when visiting different places shown on a UK weather map.
	3 Recording the weather	Using symbols and written descriptions, the children record the weather in their own area.
Towns	1 Understanding towns	The children draw three important buildings in East Kilbride and work out their grid references.
	2 The origin of towns	The children select the correct symbol for different types of town.
	3 Town life	Pupils make a survey of street furniture in the local streets.
Food and shops	1 Farms and food	Pupils make drawings of different and food and link them to their origins on a world map.
	2 From farm to supermarket	Children complete a flow line diagram showing how bananas are brought to the UK from Jamaica.
	3 Local shops	Children name local shops and decide on the type of service they provide.

Aim	Teaching point
To show that coastlines vary considerably.	Discuss the features of the different coastlines before the children choose one for a holiday.
To consolidate understanding of the different coastal features.	You might want to discuss how hard rocks resist erosion and thus form headlands.
To illustrate how people have altered the coast for their own use.	See that pupils colour the key before they complete the map.
To highlight the different features of a river system.	Pupils will need to choose six features from the picture in the pupil book.
To develop map reading skills and to highlight physical features of a river system.	Check that pupils can read specific place names such as 'Kabalega Falls' and 'Khartoum'.
To illustrate the range of jobs which need to be done to manage rivers.	You might want to discuss which job is most important before pupils write down their own answers.
To develop children's weather word vocabulary.	Extend the work by putting up a display of extreme weather events in the UK and elsewhere.
To practice using and reading weather symbols.	You could extend the work by looking at symbol weather maps of the UK.
To describe the weather using words and symbols.	Pupils could observe the weather by looking out of the window but it is much better to go outside.
To show how aerial photographs are an important source of information about places.	Check that the children are clear about how to use alpha-numeric grid references.
To reinforce the idea that towns originate in different ways.	Use the symbols in a class display of towns in your own region.
To develop local area fieldwork and awareness of different services.	You need to be aware that drawings will not always match exactly the items that the children discover.
To show how the fruit and vegetables that we eat come from many different parts of the world.	Consider the different types of transport needed to bring fruit and vegetables to the UK.
To introduce pupils to a flow diagram as a way of illustrating a process.	This activity links to the study of Jamaica in pupil book 5.
To analyse shops using categories.	When they decide where they buy things try to focus on local shops rather than a single supermarket.

Copymaster matrix

Unit	Copymaster	Description
Environment	1 Old and new buildings	Children make a drawing of how an old windmill could be restored and identify a local example.
	2 Making improvements	Children annotate drawings of different improvement schemes and select a local example.
	3 Comparing places	Children make an environmental quality survey of a local street.
Northern Ireland	1 Introducing Northern Ireland	Using an outline map of Northern Ireland, the children add features specified in a list.
	2 Living in Northern Ireland	Pupils use word lists to describe the area around Ballyknock Farm.
	3 A journey to Londonderry	The children devise a picture sequence of the O'Neill's journey to Londonderry.
Germany	1 Knowing Germany	Children complete fact files about the physical and human geography of Germany.
	2 The Ruhr: An industrial region	Pupils complete a map of the Ruhr and write a few sentences describing it.
	3 Living in Dinslaken	The children complete drawings which they link to a map of Dinslaken.
North America	1 Introducing North America	Working from a key, pupils colour different countries and regions of North America.
	2 Finding out about Canada	Pupils extract information from a map of Canada and play a dice game.
	3 Crossing the Rockies	Children make small drawings of different aspects of the Rockies to create an image box.
Asia	1 The Gulf	Pupils complete an outline map and write down three key facts about The Gulf.
	2 Introducing the United Arab Emirates	Pupils colour a traditional Islamic design and make their own drawing of the Burj Khalifa skyscraper.
	3 Exploring the United Arab Emirates	Pupils answer questions about their own lifestyles to find out about their environmental footprint.

Aim	Teaching point
To get children to think about local buildings that they value and how they could be used.	You might get pupils to draw plans to show their ideas.
To show how places can be improved and to practice making annotated drawings.	Pupils will need to visit a local site in order to complete the second activity.
To use different graphical recording devices to represent survey findings.	Check that pupils understand how to complete the profile diagram – small shapes will indicate a poor environment.
To introduce children to some of the key features of Northern Ireland.	See that pupils understand the outline map and can identify borders, seas and lakes.
To devise a place portrait using geographical vocabulary.	The word lists could be applied to your own locality to provide a contrasting portrait.
To reinforce pupils understanding of landmarks and sequence.	You will need to provide scissors, glue and strips of card.
To extend children's knowledge and understanding of Germany.	Pupils could use information from the photographs and map when they complete the 'other information' file box.
To help children develop their understanding of a major European industrial region.	Thinking about the future of the Ruhr is a challenge but it is a reminder that places are always changing.
To introduce children to a locality in Germany.	See that the children can identify the buildings shown on the outline map of Dinslaken.
To consolidate children's understanding and ability to recognise major North American countries.	Talk with pupils about how Alaska is part of the USA and that Greenland is linked to Denmark.
To help children learn about some of the key physical and human features of Canada.	Pupils could play this game in groups of four as well as in pairs.
To highlight different aspects of the Rockies in an imaginative way.	Children will need glue and scissors in order to complete this activity.
To name and identify different countries in The Gulf.	Explain that Bahrain is a small island and therefore difficult to show on the map of the whole region.
To illustrate two contrasting aspects of life in the UAE today.	There are natural links to art and design which can be developed from this activity.
To raise awareness of how the things we do impact on the natural environment.	See that the pupils understand why each of the things in the list has an environmental impact.

1 The seashore

1. Colour the pictures of the mudflats and shingle beach.

2. Draw pictures of a sandy beach and rocky coastline in the empty boxes.

3. Which one would you choose for a holiday?

   Write about your choice and make a drawing of it.

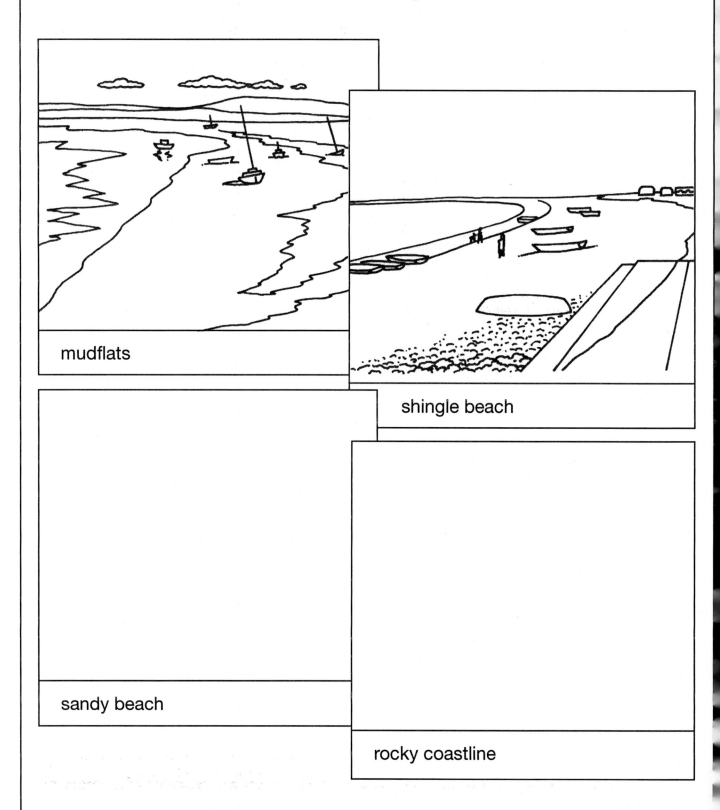

mudflats

shingle beach

sandy beach

rocky coastline

Name ....

1. Colour the key.

2. Colour the drawing using these colours.

Key	
cliffs	
sea	
beach	
grass	

3. Write a sentence about the beach.

....

....

....

1. Colour the roads, beach, sea, town, countryside and gardens on the map and key.

2. Write the words in the empty boxes where they belong.

      beach   rocks   groynes   cliff path   gardens

Key

roads	beach	sea	town	countryside	gardens
red	yellow	blue	grey	light green	dark green

1. Make a list of six features you can find along a river.

2. Write the numbers from the table on the correct part of the picture.

Features you can find along a river
1
2
3
4
5
6

5 Rivers matter

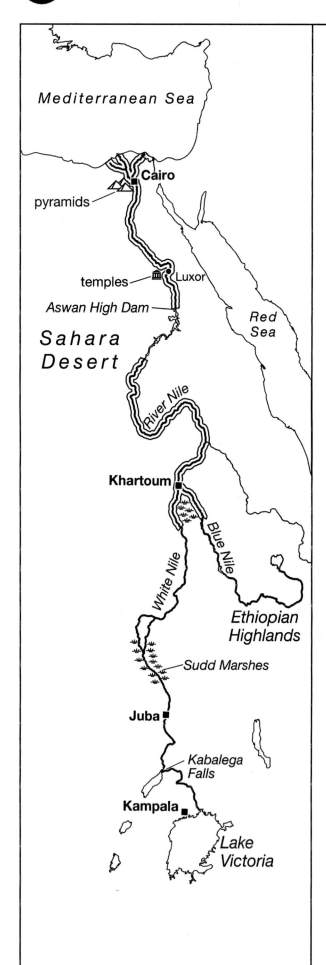

1. Colour the diagram of the River Nile and create a key to explain your diagram.

2. Working from the map, complete these sentences.

The Nile rises in the ....

....

....

The streams flow into Lake

....

The river goes through the

.... Marshes.

The Nile crosses the

.... Desert.

The Nile divides into streams

to make a ....

Key	
Sea and lakes	
Desert	
Irrigated land	
Marshes	

Name ....

1. Make drawings of the jobs which Valerie Hay and her team do.

Taking water samples	Taking soil samples
Talking to the public	Testing for pollution

2. Which job do you think is most important and why?

....

....

....

Name ....

1. Choose the best words from the word bank to go with each picture.

2. Colour each picture.

3. Which weather problem do you think lasts longest?

....

Word Bank			
dry	hot	rainy	wet
water	thirsty	windy	drowned
frightening	noisy	dust	dangerous

Hurricane	Best words

Flood	Best words

Drought	Best words

Name ....

1. Colour and label the weather symbols for sunny, rainy, and sun and cloud.

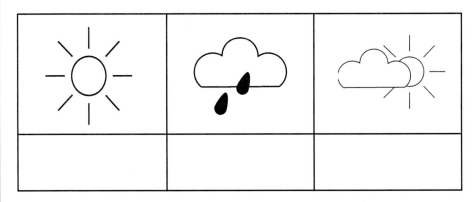

2. Colour and label the clothes.

umbrella   T shirt   boots   shorts

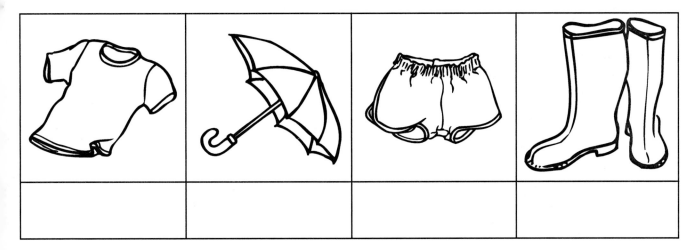

3. Using the map and symbols decide on the weather and the clothes needed for Manchester and Aberdeen.

Place	Aberdeen
Weather	
Clothes needed	

Place	Manchester
Weather	
Clothes needed	

9 **Recording the weather**   *Name* ....

1. The symbols show what the weather was like in Cardiff one day in June last year. Write a description of the weather.

2. Draw symbols and write about the weather today.

wind

temperature

cloud

....

....

....

....

wind

temperature

cloud

....

....

....

....

1. Draw pictures of three important buildings in East Kilbride.

2. Write a sentence saying why you chose each building.

3. Write down the grid square from the photograph.

1	
	....
	....
	....
	....
	....
	Grid Square [ ]
2	
	....
	....
	....
	....
	....
	Grid Square [ ]
3	
	....
	....
	....
	....
	Grid Square [ ]

11 The origin of towns

Name ....

1. Draw one of the symbols in the right circle.

2. Draw a symbol for your nearest town in the last circle.

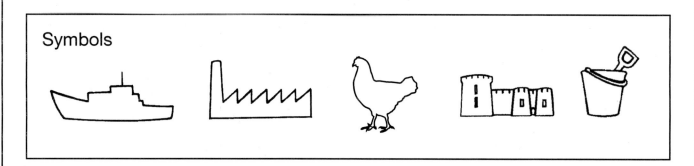

Symbols

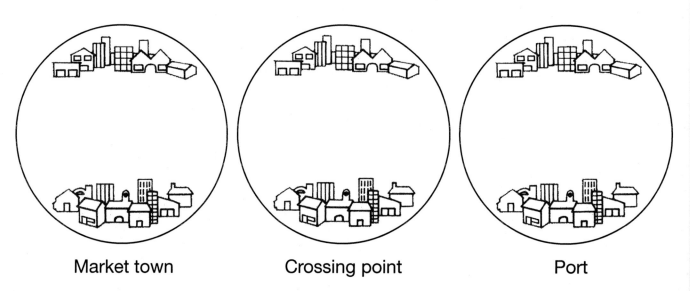

| Market town | Crossing point | Port |

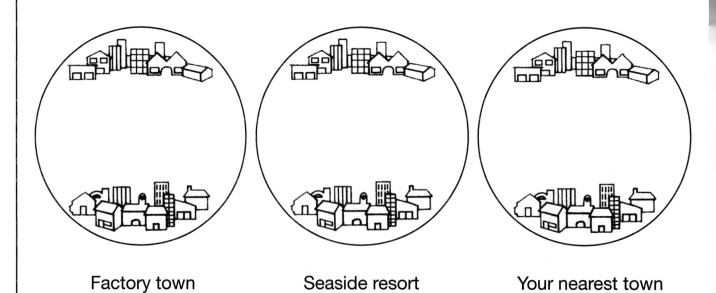

| Factory town | Seaside resort | Your nearest town |

12 Town life

1. Make a survey of the streets near your school. Tick or colour a box each time you find one of the things in the drawings.

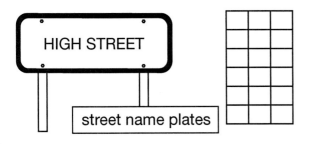

street name plates

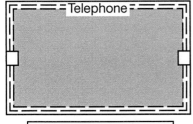

telephone covers

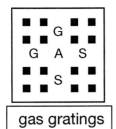

gas gratings

post boxes

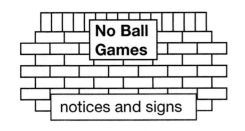

notices and signs

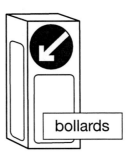

bollards

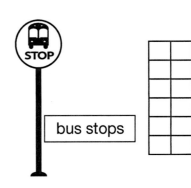

bus stops

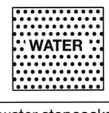 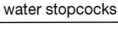

water stopcocks

fire hydrant markers

 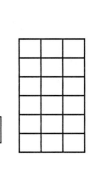

traffic signs

13 Farms and food

Name ....

1. Draw pictures in the empty boxes.

2. Draw lines from each box to the correct place on the map.

1. Grapefruit	2. Oranges	3. Tomatoes

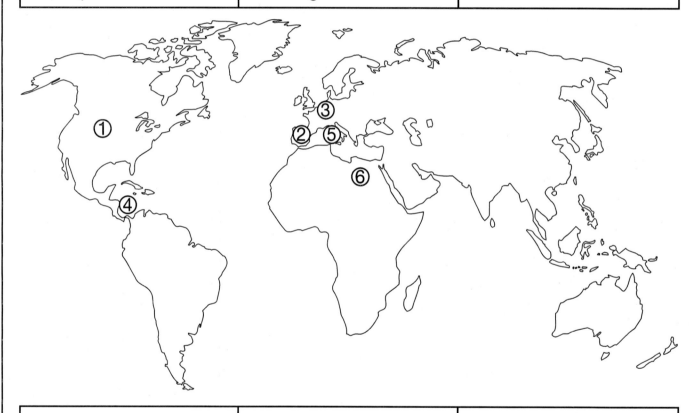

4. Bananas	5. Grapes	6. Potatoes

14 From farm to supermarket

Name ....

1. Draw pictures in the empty circles to show how bananas are imported from Jamaica.
2. Add arrows which link the pictures in the correct order.

Growing

Transporting

Packing

Distributing

Selling

15 Local shops

1. Write down the name of the shop where you would go for each of the items on the list.

2. Colour the code box using these colours.

Food	green

Money	red

Household goods	blue

Shopping list

Items needed	Name of shop	Code
Loaf of bread		
Newspaper		
Tin of baked beans		
Plasters		
Money		
Cake		
Stamps		
Sweets		
Onions		
Pet food		
Book		

Name ....

1. Colour the picture of the old windmill.

2. Draw what it would look like if it was repaired and turned into a house.

Old windmill 	Windmill today

broken sail

cracks in the bricks

door hanging from its hinges

mill stone in the grass

3. Draw a building in your area which you think should be saved for the future.

	This building is interesting because
	....
	....
	....
	....
	....
	....

17 Making improvements

1. Use the list of words to help you label the drawings.

2. Make a labelled drawing to show how a place near your school has been improved.

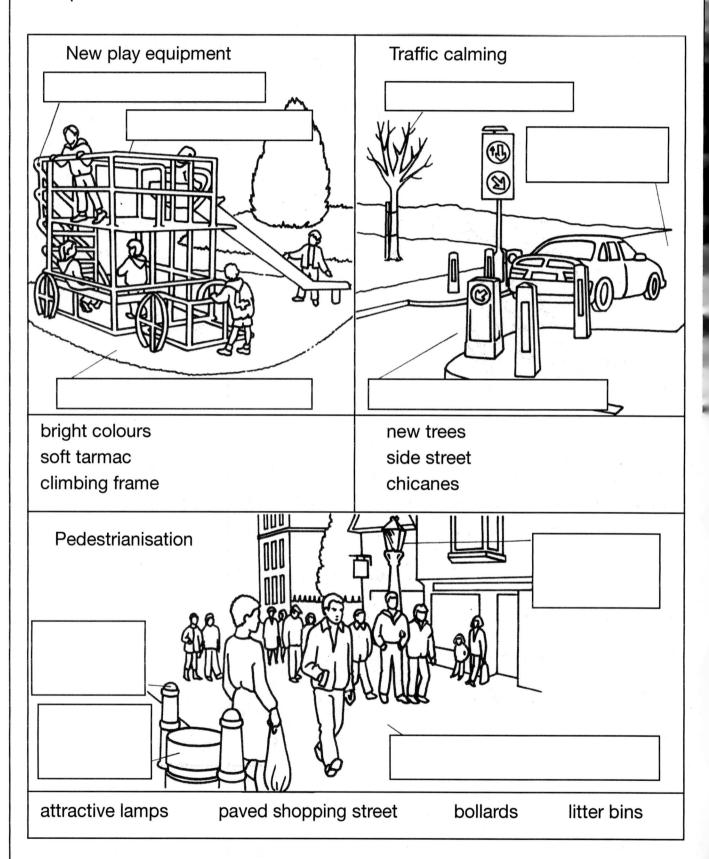

New play equipment

bright colours
soft tarmac
climbing frame

Traffic calming

new trees
side street
chicanes

Pedestrianisation

attractive lamps   paved shopping street   bollards   litter bins

Name ....

1. Make a survey of a street near your school.

   Name of street ....

2. Answer each survey question by filling in a box.

3. Show your results on the street profile.

Questions	←	1	2	3	4	5	→
Litter	A lot of litter						Very clean
Noise	A lot of noise						Very quiet
Air	Air bad to breathe						Clean, fresh air
Buildings	In poor repair						In good repair
Plants	No trees or gardens						Plenty of plants
Safety	Lots of dangers						Very safe
Wires	A lot of ugly aerials						No wires
Pavements	Uneven, poor repair						Clean and smooth

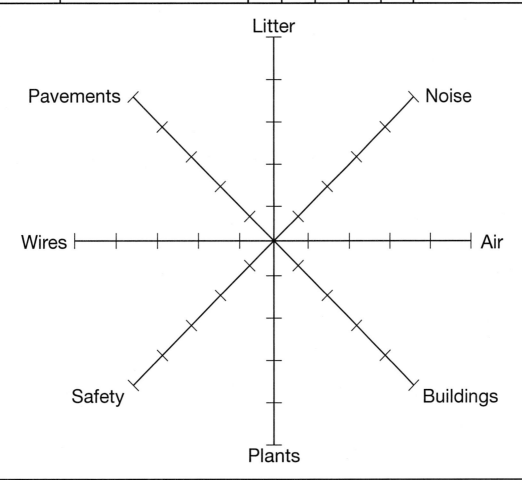

⑲ Introducing Northern Ireland

Name ....

1. Mark these places on the map of Northern Ireland.

   Londonderry (Derry)   River Bann   Sperrin Mountains

   Lough Neagh   Antrim Mountains   Belfast

   Mourne Mountains   Irish Sea

2. Colour the sea, rivers and lakes blue, the border red and the land green.

NORTHERN IRELAND

IRELAND

20 Living in Northern Ireland

Name ....

1. Look at each group of words in turn. Colour the circles next to the words which describe the area around Ballyknock Farm.

Landscape	
cliff	○
coast	○
flat	○
hill	○
lake	○
marsh	○
mountain	○
river	○
slope	○
valley	○

Buildings	
church	○
factory	○
garage	○
hospital	○
hotel	○
house	○
inn	○
office	○
school	○
shop	○

Transport	
aeroplane	○
bike	○
bus	○
car	○
ferry	○
lorry	○
motorbike	○
ship	○
train	○
underground	○

Land use	
car park	○
farm	○
gardens	○
housing	○
industry	○
park	○
playground	○
road	○
wasteland	○
wood	○

Employment	
bus driver	○
butcher	○
dentist	○
doctor	○
greengrocer	○
librarian	○
postman	○
secretary	○
shopkeeper	○
teacher	○

Environment	
attractive	○
clean	○
dirty	○
dull	○
interesting	○
noisy	○
quiet	○
smelly	○
ugly	○
untidy	○

2. Write a short report about what the dots tell you.

   Primary Geography Pupil Book 4: Northern Ireland pp38-43

21 **A journey to Londonderry** *Name* ....

1. Make your own drawings in the empty boxes

2. Cut out the drawings.

3. Glue the drawings on to a strip of card in the order that the O'Neill's saw them.

Ballyknock Farm

Ness Wood

Dungiven Castle

Glenshane Pass

Londonderry

1. Complete the Fact Files on rivers, weather, cities and work in Germany.

2. Write a few sentences giving information about Germany.

Rivers
1
2
3
4

Weather
Winter
Wind

Cities
1
2
3
4
5

Work

Other information

23 **The Ruhr: An industrial region**   *Name* ....

1. Label the towns and colour the map of the Ruhr.

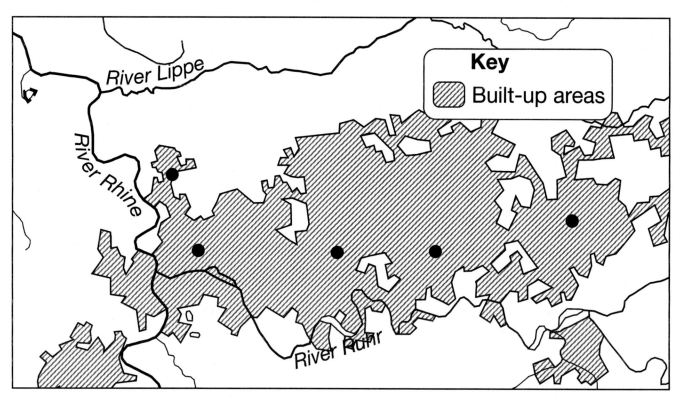

2. Write a few sentences about the Ruhr in the past, present and future.

....

....

....

....

....

....

....

....

....

....

Name ....

1. Draw Dominic's grandmother's house in the empty box.

2. Colour and label the two other drawings.

3. Draw a line from each picture to the correct place on the map.

Grandmother's house

1. Colour the key.

2. Name and colour the countries on the map.

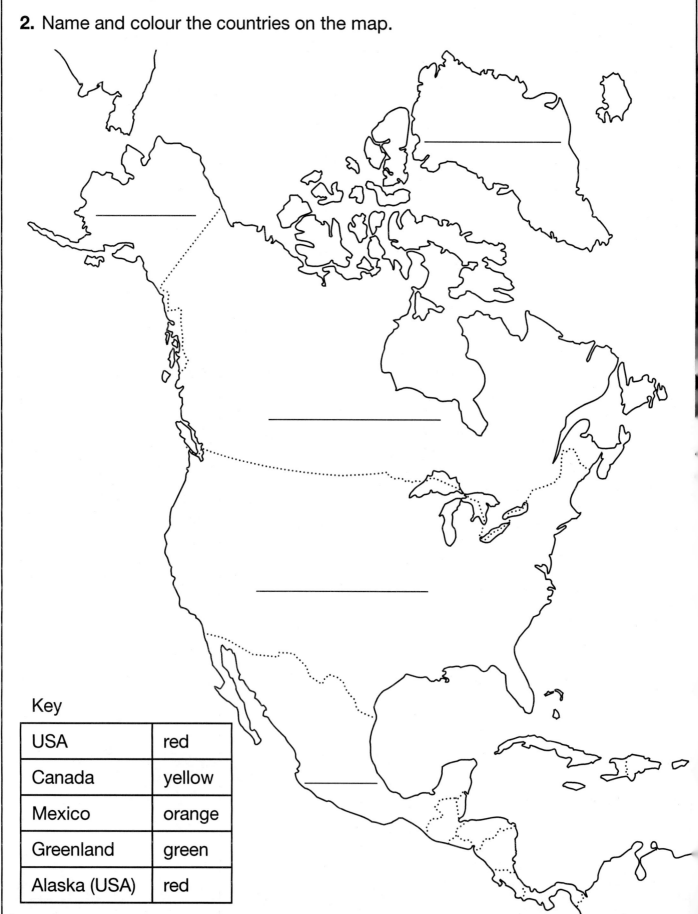

Key

USA	red
Canada	yellow
Mexico	orange
Greenland	green
Alaska (USA)	red

1. Write the names of the places on the map in the table.

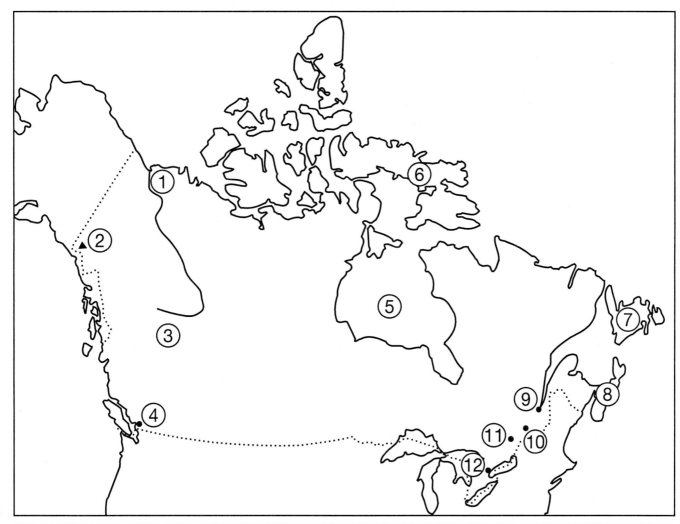

① Mackenzie River	⑦
②	⑧
③	⑨
④	⑩
⑤	⑪
⑥	⑫

2. Now play a game with someone else. You will need two dice and 12 counters each. Throw the dice in turns and put a counter on the map for each number that you throw, the first player to put down all their counters wins.

27 **Crossing the Rockies**

Name ....

1. Draw pictures and colour each square of the cube.

2. Cut around the edge of the cube.

3. Fold along the lines and glue down the flaps to make your model.

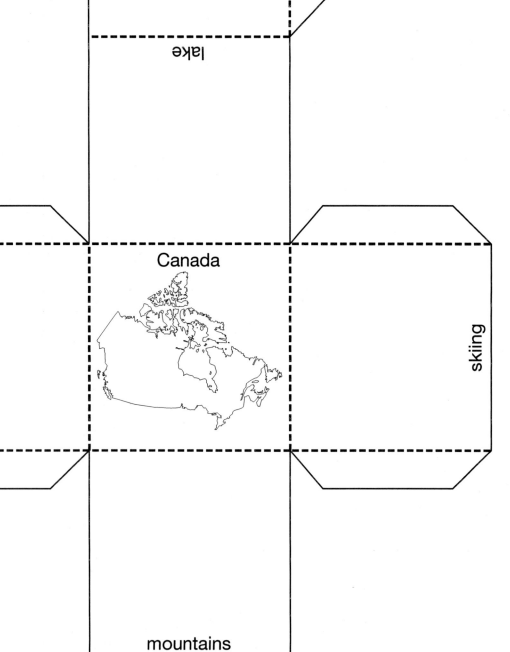

forest

lake

bear

Canada

skiing

mountains

Name ....

1. Name the countries numbered on the map.

2. Colour the map using blue for the sea.

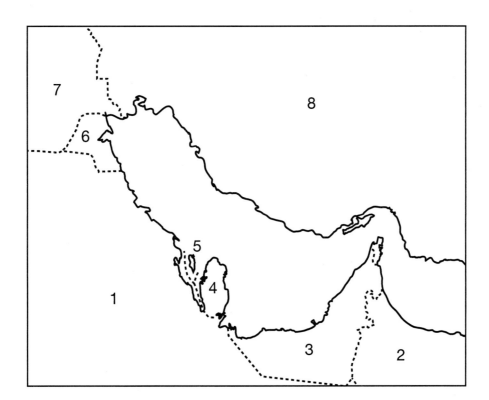

1		5	
2		6	
3		7	
4		8	

3. Write down what you think are the three most important facts about The Gulf.

Fact 1	Fact 2	Fact 3

1. Colour the pattern.

2. Now draw the tallest building in the world.

3. Make up a sentence about each drawing.

....

....

....

Name ....

1. Find out about your environmental footprint by completing this survey. Colour a dot for each thing you do.

   Be honest!

Shopping	Do you?
Get a plastic bag each time you shop?	○
Mostly buy frozen food?	○
Never look to see where food comes from?	○
Get rid of toys and clothes before they wear out?	○

Waste	Do you?
Throw all rubbish in the same bin?	○
Sometimes drop litter?	○
Sometimes leave food at mealtimes?	○
Sometimes keep taps running?	○

Energy	Do you?
Turn up the heat rather than put on extra clothes?	○
Sometimes forget to turn off lights?	○
Go on car journeys when you could walk?	○
Leave doors open quite often?	○

Leisure	Do you?
Watch a lot of TV?	○
Sit about a lot?	○
Use quite a lot of batteries?	○
Travel by aeroplane?	○

2. For each dot you have filled in colour a space green on the REASONABLE footprint.

3. Colour extra squares red on the UNREASONABLE footprint if you need extra spaces.

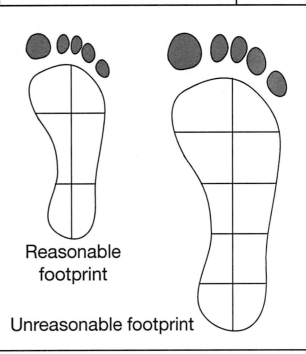

Reasonable footprint

Unreasonable footprint

Geography in the English National Curriculum

A new primary geography curriculum was introduced in England in 2014. This new curriculum provides a framework for schools to follow but leaves teachers considerable scope to select and organise the content according to their individual needs. It should also be noted that the curriculum is only intended to occupy a proportion of the school day and that schools are free to devise their own studies in the time that remains.

Purpose of study

The aim of geographical education is clearly articulated in the opening section of the Programme of Study which states:

A high quality geography education should inspire in pupils a curiosity and fascination about the world and its people that will remain with them for the rest of their lives. Teaching should equip pupils with knowledge about diverse places, people, resources and natural and human environments, together with a deep understanding of the Earth's key physical and human processes. As pupils progress, their growing knowledge about the world should help them to deepen their understanding of the interaction between physical and human processes, and of the formation and use of landscapes and environments. Geographical knowledge, understanding and skills provide the frameworks and approaches that explain how the Earth's features at different scales are shaped and interconnected and change over time.

Subject content

The National Curriculum provides the following general guidance for each Key Stage:

Key Stage 1
Pupils should develop knowledge about the world, the United Kingdom and their locality. They should understand basic subject-specific vocabulary relating to human and physical geography and begin to use geographical skills, including first-hand observation, to enhance their locational awareness.

Key Stage 2
Pupils should extend their knowledge and understanding beyond the local area to include the United Kingdom and Europe, North and South America. This will include the location and characteristics of a range of the world's most significant human and physical features. They should develop their use of geographical knowledge, understanding and skills to enhance their locational and place knowledge.

Teachers who are familiar with the previous version of the curriculum will note the increasing emphasis on factual and place knowledge. For example, there is a greater focus on learning about the UK and Europe. Map reading and communication skills are also highlighted. On the other hand, there are no specific references to the developing world and sustainability is not mentioned directly. However, there is an expectation that schools will work from the Programmes of Study to develop a broad and balanced curriculum which meets the needs of learners in their locality. This provides schools with scope to enrich the curriculum and rectify any omissions which they may perceive.

Key Stage 2 Programme of study

The elements specified in the Key Stage 2 programme of study are listed below. The summary provided here should read alongside the statements about the wider aims of the curriculum. There is no suggestion that pupils should work to individual statements.

Focus
Extend knowledge of UK, Europe and North and South America
Location of world's most significant human and physical features
Knowledge, understanding and skills to enhance locational and place knowledge
Locational knowledge
Locate the world's countries
Use maps to focus on countries, cities and regions in Europe
Use maps to focus on countries, cities and regions in North America
Use maps to focus on countries, cities and regions in South America
Name and locate counties of the UK
Name and locate cities of the UK
Geographical regions of the UK
Topographical features of the UK
Changing land use patterns of the UK
Significance of latitude and longitude
Significance of Equator, Northern and Southern Hemisphere, Tropics of Cancer/Capricorn, Arctic/Antarctic circles, Prime Meridian
Time zones
Day and night
Place knowledge
Regional study within UK
Regional study in a European country
Regional study in North America
Regional study in South America
Human and physical geography
Climate zones
Biomes and vegetation belts
Rivers and mountains
Volcanoes and earthquakes
Water cycle
Types of settlement and land use
Economic activity including trade links
Distribution of natural resources including energy, food, minerals, water
Skills and fieldwork
Use maps, atlases, globes and digital mapping
Use eight points of the compass
Use four and six figure grid references
Use symbols and keys (including OS maps)
Fieldwork skills

WORLD MAP

WORLD COUNTRIES

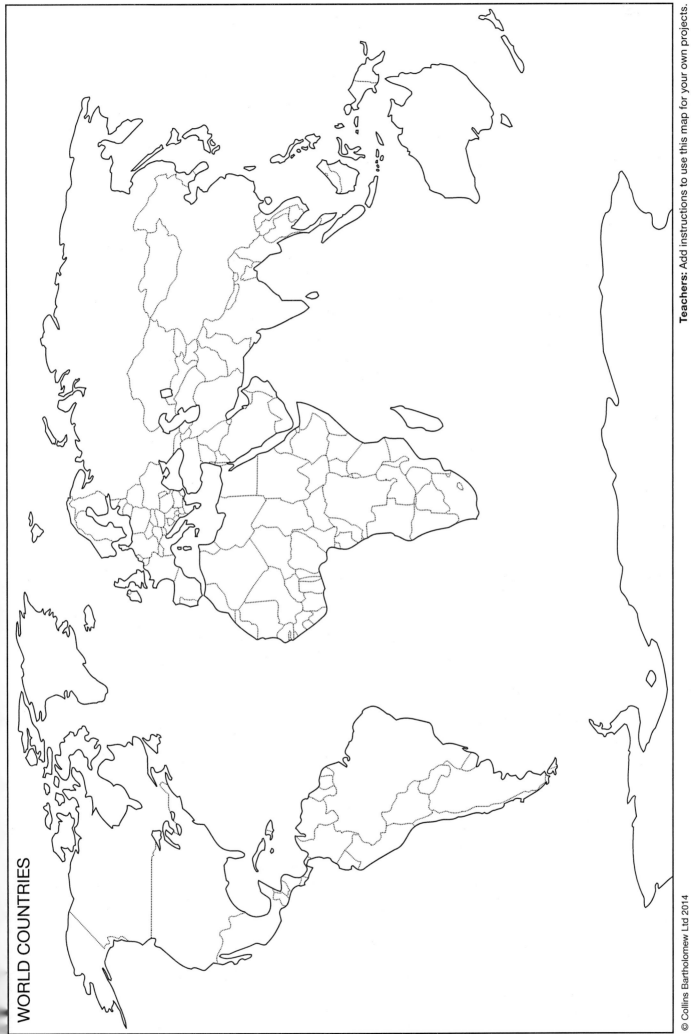

Teachers: Add instructions to use this map for your own projects.

Primary Geography Teacher's Book 4
Collins
An imprint of HarperCollins Publishers
Westerhill Road
Bishopbriggs
Glasgow
G64 2QT

ISBN 978-0-00-756365-4

Imp 001

British Library Cataloguing in Publication Data
A catalogue record for this book is available from the British Library.

Printed by RR Donnelley at Glasgow, UK.

Acknowledgements

Additional original input by Terry Jewson

Cover designs Steve Evans illustration and design

Illustrations by Jouve Pvt Ltd pp 31, 38

Photo credits:

All images from www.shutterstock.com